A taqsim is an improvisational Middle Eastern medley in which the musician moves between formal musical structure and free-flowing improvisation. In *Taqsim* Zaid Shlah writes within the formal structure of the lyric, but incorporates an innovative lyricism that agitates between his Iraqi and Canadian heritage: a history of music, food, war and love in a space as wide as the mountains and prairies of his native Alberta to as far away as the land between the two rivers, the Tigris and the Euphrates.

TAQSIM

Zaid Shlah

Frontenac House
Calgary, Alberta

Book and cover design: Epix Design
Cover photo: Photographer unknown. The publisher and author have
been unable to identify the photographer. Future editions will make full
acknowledgement if possible.
Author photo: Mark Gould

Library and Archives Canada Cataloguing in Publication
Shlah, Zaid
        Taqsim / Zaid Shlah. -- 1st Canadian ed.
Poems.
ISBN 1-897181-08-6
        I. Title.
PS8637.H53T37 2006   C811'.6   C2006-904777-4

We acknowledge the support of the Canada Council for the Arts which last
year invested $20.3 million in writing and publishing throughout Canada. We
also acknowledge the support of The Alberta Foundation for the Arts.

Canada Council **Conseil des Arts**
for the Arts **du Canada**

Alberta
Foundation
for the **Arts**

Printed and bound in Canada
Published by Frontenac House Ltd.
1138 Frontenac Avenue S.W.
Calgary, Alberta, T2T 1B6, Canada
Tel: 403-245-2491   Fax: 403-245-2380
editor@frontenachouse.com   www.frontenachouse.com

I have been fortunate enough to have several positive influences in my life: to the writers and musicians, both past and present, I am indebted to your legacy; to my dear family and friends, both in Calgary and the Bay Area, especially – the laughter.

To the many teachers who have helped me along the way: in particular, Richard Harrison, whose friendship, criticism and support has been essential to my development as a writer. And to Paul Hoover, whose many suggestions and comments helped me to carve the exacting phrase.

To my mother and father, my sister and brother, you have been relentless pillars of wisdom, support, and love. To HGS, who remains.

And to my wife, Randa, for everything that you are, for your constant support and advice, your energy and your spirit, I am blessed to have you in my life.

For my Father, ZGS

Contents

Taqsim

Leave the window, leave
the poplar, leave the clouds,
the blue tinged by sun –

leave the spruce and its cobalt
line, leave the crow and the magpie,
leave intentions and reflections, leave
the bodies as they pass, leave the couch,
leave the river, leave the grass, leave the
gaze – it's not to know; leave listlessness –
it grows too much, leave the words
rooting in your eye, leave the sun
and leave its lie –

go and be something beautiful
before you're eclipsed

≈

and I was, fingertips
           head long, foot long
into the night, keys
like William Carlos Williams,
I danced the
           cerebral light –

my Opus,
           my Magnum
needs coffee,
           and a bagel –

           but the buffoon
in blue pajamas, off to ply
the brie & red ripe sliced
tomato,

           a handsome
bowl of kalamata olives, sweet
muscat, & butter sated on a crusty
roll,

no *taqsim*, or 12 yr
scotch to bring me back,

my Opus,
           my Magnum

leaks,

           and all of the
instruments, great winter
throated poplar, bare –

so how to strum it?

⁓

and there is this
darling Shahrazad, slips in
and out of frame,

pictures never got all of
her, the colour of her skin, her
ass shifting in the low-lit room,

    line of thigh drummed
between my fingers – evenings where
she danced like
          a gypsy –

    her body rocking and falling like animals
at night, her salt-skin dripping with rough circles,
and every muscle fighting to drive her further away

    what footprint,
        what hip-song,

    the picture, or
watching her move out to
places my body has never
been

≈

given,

given
   to weight,

      even "goodnight,"
            is thick,

            I walk past her room,
      I can hear her; she's got Christ
      out again –

         creeps out of her room to
      remind me, a petrified ghost;

she looks up at me, and then
God, her voice shaking in Arabic,

*"Allah towul umrek, Allah nagihuk,
corbanic,"* hands quaking in alms.

"goodnight," I kiss her, "good night"

she turns, continues to pray,

         *"Allah towul umrek,
         Allah nagihuk, corbanic,"*

               "goodnight,"
            "goodnight"

∼

youthful literati:
    a child's *taqsim*[1] –

"fly fly fly red wagon fly
down by the green worm, and all the
way down, fly wagon fly"

    magician
of these neighborhood streets, spills
out the order of syllables, never to be
repeated –

    later, he etches the cryptic marks
on paper, the A's & B's carefully codified
into secret ticks and hoops,

    more concerned with
the look of the thing, the artifice of letter
breathes in him – out; who is whose keeper?

    buzzing like flies to those
records on 45 rpm instead of 33; the
high pitched squeaks,

    as he hollers out names
inspired by Dr. Seuss: Eugene Snuffin-
box & Marvin Moon Balloon Face –

(and what does it all mean?)

as he busts his guts
    out laughing

    ∼

years later,
the prof going on about William
Blake and his use of the colour red,

and red continues in strands
about her hair – I've never slept
with a red-head before,

and what the hell were they
all up on, these faces in the classroom,
paprika-sun, or a red wheelbarrow?

as red "runs in
blood down palace walls" –

and the guy next to me, his eyes
awash in the torpor of a sun drawn
afternoon,
                    red riding hood
skipping in verse, of a girl he
once kissed –

and this picture of a
boy whose father reads aloud,
"red dog, see the red dog run,"

suddenly the boy
says "red dog" and his father
kisses him & hugs him,

what stays,
                    whatever remains,

and what red hue
will be reeling years from now
when this boy, a young man, sits
down to read from the poetry of
William Blake?

≈

Poem from Istanbul

I heard the hands
of a Turkish man

speaking Greek
to a woman

of such fine elderly
proportion

one could have seen
in her youth how Helen
begat war –

better I turn my head towards
the window, and watch the rain
fall on Istanbul

≈

to make your way to that island,
where a simple wooden shed stands
handsome in the sun,

and a rough coat like a sailor's,
and a few of your books and a pen;

where your days consist of your time
by the light of the window, and you are
left to become a thing of your own –

         the simple bed that lies
next to you, the bread, and the butter,
and the chickens out back –

where the lives of the fishermen
and the poet seem to be one; living
for the catching of fish, or a well
crafted line

≈

among the three women
                stopped for lunch,
        nearly two centuries
        of life, a small Mediterranean cafe;

kibi balls of bulgur wheat, filo pastry
stuffed with spiced meat, and in three small
glasses, brown ale stood neat –

sipping comfortably, mid-speech – Arabic
gutturals and rolling R's moved through shoulders
and eyebrows, arms and fingers moved as fish
might at sea;

how they seemed like their jewelry
formed from the earth, like their words
over time; their language pressed into
their skin

     ~

days I spent
with Musa and Asim,

then the tourists
    would come –

        "Sitting here,

        "Yes, it's nice

        "Twenty dollars gets
        you lunch on a Persian rug
        by the river"

        "Really" "Yes

            "No, thank you."

            that this is my orient,
my tourist stand, my Musa and Asim,
my chai, and my saz^2

later, during the night, I'd go back
to the terrace of my motel, watch the

                                    gophers

        shimmy indifferently
            across Pigeon Valley

                notes like
        cardamom and all-spice

$\sim$

come out of the corners of the shadowy room,
the Asik[3] plays the oud with the men seated
round him, taking tiny sips from their arak[4] ;

Nana's house brims with the smell
of sweet dough, her great hips in the center
of the kitchen working the stove,

later filling the cups with dark chai,
then with boiling water from the larger
kettle beneath;

       notes like cardamom
         and all-spice

       and as I help her to bring
out the plate of *ca'ick* and *lowzina*, she
urges us all to eat; and we all eat, and taste
and drink

       neither caring nor
wondering why the Asik's song
is bittersweet

≈

but tonight, I like a duck –
        to go drinking with
ducks,

fuck the moon, and chase
half-crazy women –

        Leyla, ruby wine,
or Suzanne down by the
river,

        Sappho's
words like gilded
cormorants,

and my pockets stuffed
with cash, but no Helen –

there's Circe, surpassingly
beautiful, but not one wing'ed
word to entreat her,

                last call
for a jovial tune, my duck
haphazardly over the jocund
moon,

& turning, to bid him
good evening,

                crash down
                from feigned
                        Eden,
        leaks,

from my ears,
        spills from my nose

∼

Requirements before leaving:

That leaving you will be easier than
your leaving me, that the bridges will
have blown up only after I have crossed
them, that the house on my back will
keep like a camel, that air will not run
out, that I am defective, and so too is
the world, that together we will be wholly
defective, that the old man's beads I
shape between my fingers: shiny new
words, that I fit love with a brand new
pair of boots, and then walk on my hands,
that mother and father will disown me,
that I will become unwritten, a godless
grain of sand, that I will sleep less, dream
more, speak without "will be" and "have
to", that on the going, a celebration: spit
cooked lamb served whole, heaps of rice
mixed with pine nuts, wine, and a concussion
from which to wake, largely displaced

≈

The return

I first sought clarinet evenings,
exquisite after three of the moon,
the world gone down into splinters,
borne up on Iznik palmettos I would
have served to you in the Arabic,
tammar, jibben abyeth u ghaweh,
but that's over now, returned to the
comfort of the old panegyric circles,
Babylon, its tired tower, the apocalypse,
and that God was also ours; greetings
John, Saul, and your blinding flash
of light – Mohummed I await your
last call, ashes to ashes, and all that ash
in between we never could clear, in the
end, it isn't so much a departure, as

a step into
the familiar

            his footsteps shifting
over cobblestones, hands clasped
behind him, progressing like the lines
of a dignified poem –

for another mouthful, an unfinished
dream, for nothing – a body moving in
skin; and how many stones have you
met with old man?

and if you ask me why I love him,
I will only have this to give you: that in
a dream, you and I will sit together;

I get up to reach for the kettle,
filling it with water, setting it to boil
as we talk small things: the house, the
weather, the week, and things to come,

with the sounds of bubbling filling the
room, I rise to fix the coffee – two heaping
spoonfuls of the dark ground bean,

blow down on the black foam
erupting from the kettle, gently stirring
in the sugar to sweeten; then after a time,
pouring the rich brew into hand embroidered
cups, spun from clay collected near a river
in Anatolia, older than pottery, older

and as we step out into the dying sex
of Autumn, with you asking me to teach you
next time, wind undressing the long branches
of the willow, the apple tree promenading its
red treasure, and twilight just coming on –
maybe, if you sit still, and sip lightly like
I do, this will be answer enough

    ～

do you think when he rose up over the mountains,
sword held high over an Arabian horse, with Allah
on the move, and ten thousand Bedouin behind him,
charging in a vision

do you think he had any idea that the force
that drove him across the desert that year, would drive
an empire across three continents; did he know of the
splendor that would come to that learned city of Baghdad;
did he know of the crimes that would come after the
Mongols sacked her?

did Caesar's legionnaires, did the Byzantine, did Alexander
and the Greek, did the Ottoman? And 500 yrs before Plato sang
his songs an Assyrian King rode into Babylonia on a golden
chariot decrying the false gods and erecting the new, and did
he know that he too would rise to fall, shine and then fade?

I wonder when our Americas will fall, and then I begin
to think about my empire of thigh and torso, my congress
of mind; what force will bring decay to my walls of sinew,
my pillars of bone – will I go lame, my mind sift to dust?

now in the sun of my life, how should I
go about building my armies of flesh, my
songs of movement, my legacy of love,
what great river should my body
carve out?

∼

"Before I get up
I check to see if I'm in a state
of grace –

and if I am, I get up,
if not, I go back to bed,"

and those are the words
            of the poet that hit me;

starting out   before the Aegean Sea,
                muscles slipped against the waves
for the current, and I am a thousand miles
            from home,

                    maybe a thousand
            words from the shore,

and I have never been
much of a swimmer, but here in a
bowl of the sun,

            a small god
                        dying

                    the waves feeding me
                            salt and then brine,

            muscles slipped for
                        the current

∼

drinking the *maqam*[5]
    of the great Iraqi singer,

    moved to
sip *mistakhe*, white

or wind through
        hollow reeds,

    goes
as gutters go,

 old man,
whose words? –

    after all, the
cobblestones saw to it,

        long before you or
I could place them – hurts,

our feet bent against the
        grooves,

fingers clenched deep
into her belly, as if to hold on,

        as if needing,
at least the dirt,

        great winter
throated poplar, bare –

            but never a thing
                apart,

taqsim

            ends or
                it begins

Impressions from the East

Afternoon's Confession

I sat, Heidegger sat, my wife
leaving and left us, ensconced
comfortably, on the green
green lawn,

corpuscular, textiles from the Silk Road, mute
things of all kinds, Aramaic off the Arab ear, a
leaf in tiny fragments nests in the matter of eye,
but nothing moves, Pangea, nor the tides,

ring in sentient things, icicles of different
note, this is or isn't oscillation, the utterance peeled
back from the sentence, in search of a sound that fits,

I confess, I murder history, usurp the days & nights
inside the minutiae of scalpel, yet slighter still, a hair,
shard of a hair, a shadow stalks the ebb of meniscus

in pastel gray, and all of the animals, cormorant
& crane, and migrant pink flamingo, a moose must
spray its musk, and reindeer elks the night,

hay bales hum their wind-blown days, a
farmer plants philosophy, the unripened vine,
stitch & cortex resonate, not in symbols, nor

are these cymbals adequately played, but drills
alone for the oil that is, and sifts to page, a poem in
English, nobody reads a heartbeat, tinge of marmalade

drips from the sky, so subtle, so subtle it creeps,
fingers on raw wine tulips, melt-white, and ice dawned
pelicans tinker off the instruments like leggy ants

red and incongruous, nocturnal tiles, shades of apex,
tibia & femur, masons or guilds, builders of cells or prisons,
freedom in a raven's eye, garlanded girl, and golden braid

white cheese, *abyath*, *tammar*, dates, *gulbi*, my love,
the space between A and B, Heidegger's midnight orange,
now I see tangential honey, almond sun, and orange peels

off mandolins, orchestral tea, there's a schism
in my headroom, this torture of the cortex begs
for deference, like light through church stained

glass, the bobbing and going, a black bishop
coiled in Syriac, how to escape this couch, this
hymnal-heavy book, this Al-Cazar of sound, mass

marched ubiquitous, so many lyrics marched out
into the Syrian sun, and Saladin has a picture there,
stands tantamount, these rhymes in stiff iambics

without ghazal or chance to find a form, give me
Greek, or isle of Rhodos, tear down linguistics, the
right to confer a poem with all the mental resin

of Tiberius' discordant modes, as if primordial,
before the lurch of dawn, the first period, before
predicate & lofty prose, I saw Samarkand

at war, withdraw its sword, a crow will peck
its eyes, this snow will ice and muezzin will sound atop
this minaret – *Allah u akbar* – *merhaba, zane,* and

hear this howl oud, the Taurus Mountains occupy
the Northern landscape of my brain, and weightless
as a pod of Orcas at the bottom of the Arctic Sea

drowned out by Bach's 6 cello suites, and
Heidegger read Nietzsche whom I ate, I take my
gin & whiskey neat, to cool the storm, delineate

waves, this my sarcophagus, a bulging chord,
won't burst, not now, rides in Timor from Turkmenistan,
a colour more severe than iron-ore, and rapes a city &

all its verse tossed into the Shat el Arab, a funeral
grave for dying pictures, rise in plumes of oil sketches,
these Eastern dishes of cream and butter, *cagik* &

hummus, a dish of monumental onions, woven
zahferon & fresh mint tea, crisp fried eggplant – tired,
sat sitting, bloated by this feast, a brick of prisoners

without resolve to break, glass bottom boat
too far out now to paint the scene, and my wife
has just returned, I must confess, not having
stirred, or done a thing all day.

Occident to Orient

1

but I wanted to know you,
what progress I could find there,
show you snow, proffer bushels
of snow, white – and no apricots;

I wanted you to sound lovingly,
mahogany oud, because I had
come all this way, and my ship
leaves tomorrow –

resolutions drawn up from
the other side of the ocean
argue for the aesthetic of a girl
with eyes like plums, black
and sad,

and as the drums begin
to beat, the taste of anise
on our tongues,

almond shells left on
the Persian rug – this
Arabic, I find, is easy

2

I saw her, the cotton rags
about her, torn – her shoes barely
covering her tiny feet

and I wanted to save her, to
run out and steal her, shelve
her in some ivory room, away
from all this ugliness –

put her there, keep me here,
and this is my wanting, she feeds
me with the hunger in her belly,
and tomorrow, being a foreigner,
I must return back home

3

in a picture inside my daydreams
I enter every night, dark, with music
from the Orient

her body waiting on
the bedroom floor; my entrance,
her greeting, unmoved –

I remove thigh and chest from
its linen and cloth container, sip Ceylon
chai from an austere cup, which I have
removed from her silk & gold

my hand well within her grasp,
Napoleon's sweep and brash brigade,
not taken –

and I would sleep
for a time – this seraglio
for a bedroom;

would, that you
and I had this, and
nothing more,

I might take
you, for my bride

4

words like feathers I have plucked
from your mouth: cardamom, *zahferon,*
u sukar; and what about the labyrinth
negligee you whirl,

and the giants you placate, is this
mine or yours to bear? still, there is no
rationale –

hips, arms and thighs, palms over
Baghdad continue to sway, breasts sweeter
than dates – *arak*, white, in delicate glass

the Caliphate, and all the Arabian horses
could not stop us, almond green eyes, green
and given to dance, given to us, given; and all
you are is dance

Letters to a Young Bride

"My girl,"

and that this will have pleased
you, is not enough, will provoke the
scoffers into fits of rage, for what
ownership have I over you, to what end
does your pacified self serve mine? and
this is no defense, but that you broke free,
allowed me gentry status that afternoon
under a redwood in Bothe State Park,
you jarred the lines of symmetry,
slugged rapture from the sauvignon,
left grocers' chocolate on the rim, the
cork still floating, pushed in by my
tremulous hands, you softened and
warmed, to produce from my pocket
this ring.

"Dear,"

the whole of you
lying complacent inside
that couch of a word
worries me

that the propped pillow
of *hun*, softening at my neck,
might slip into two deferent
bodies angling for sleep

you recall that afternoon
spent shooting tequila over
warm beer

creaking into the
bookstore's basement
to slur each other love

saying our first
goodnight, then staying
the night instead –

amazing the sound
of my *name*, how it leapt
from your arabic tongue

The Reception

I

outside the ancient blue
walls of a Chaldean church
an Iraqi girl has been murdered –
         her black furrowed brow
    imbues the hot sky

II

two lovers, coiled
warm and sticky, interlaced
sea-horses, arm & thigh in the
briny sea-salt, star-fish, star-
angels, wet-damp hair,
two bodies imbue
         a white ceiling,

outside,
a crowd gathers for a
reception in San Ramon

III

what drink could separate
orange taffeta from jiggly flesh;
bring eyes, misguided, home,

bridge klutz to his
waltz, tux & tails to his
song,

ladies-a-partisan to peri-
winkle and rhyme, what love,
or palpable night, what drink

could sever fat little
man from icing tart, or
wedge of lime from
gin & ice

Arabic Snow

1

He sings as if the girl
with black eyes, the distance
between us

from the Arabic
into Canada, the Aurora
               Borealis,

its snow
          sounds lovely, this Arctic
ear, my ambassador waits for
sound

               and there is this odd frame,
it hangs on the wall, old man, he wears –
sherwal – bank notes, Turkiye, a small boy,

        though, I have never concerned myself with the finer
        details of the song, only sound and distillates of a boy
        and a flute looking vaguely at the white snow steps,
        and the old man walking into the foreground –

        not entirely Bedouin, yet,
        everything is where it ought
        to be

        there is mother & father
at the window, the minuscule of ice
coats pane, tongues stick crystallite,
and Nathem al-Ghazali
                    wails

        a nebulas tune, a

brown girl, door opens to freezer
night, another beer chinks glass – cold
with ice chips

somebody's out on the
phone crossing Damascene
light,

his wounds
wail over the moon

2

There's a house serves
ripe dates, short distance
from a poplar –

winter skies pluck
a soft oud
            sound,

and we emerge
as muffled history,

        Anatolia on
shaggy Mongolian
horses,

the breath
from our ice,

and there is more warmth
here than all of the heaps of
butter steamed rice –

a girl, knee-high, with
half-empty baskets, rides

alone, she has come
from the market,

magpies prairie dots, sad
horns blow off the Bosphorous
Sea –

my brother, we are here,
with Farid El Atrash, the
forest sings to night –

upstairs, in the bedroom,
all the coats from the
new Syrian wives

there's Mom, sings
with Sabbah's *dimbuk*,

as voices stomp the worn
argyle carpet, the Ottoman
turn to the music of the Abbasid
Caliphs

Aunts turn our Uncles
because the *debkee* insists,
and feasting is best after
laps rink the ice-skates

Brocade Qanoun[6]

She comes,
bemoans the spectacle
of decanter against the
wall; insists that it be
made just

        in its placement,
there is the aperture to consider,
manner of crystal, it must be held within
certain parameters of taste, you do not add
wine, or it becomes a sullied thing, it's not meant
to work in the way of a rose – must be pruned
of its unkempt arrangements,

even ice must have its exacting
compromise, or the whole thing is a
spent ordeal, and she'll have none of it –

        she undoes
the crass participle as it offends her,
a cube or two will do, mind the hands though,
watch for the filth of the human hand –

        finish it there,
and if the thing has anything innate, – snowflakes
from the inkwell of Allah,

        she wants
for a synchronous gesture, for the
magistrate verb, won't give way to
the licentious syllable, she redefines it,
and the tug of her in me, more or less,
        us
at times, the whole

thing's a convulsive
        dirge –

                I swore to close
    my headroom on the fallout of these subjects, the
    gravity of manner weighs in, no more for beauty,
    or a well placed decanter,

                    to simpler things, a man in a tunic,
        bellowing along the shores of the
                                Euphrates,
    or families gathered on small islands singing songs in the
    middle of this river, a gazelle, or some blasted incarnation,
    flakes of Glenn Gould, or splinters wind, a moth in mute
    gestation –

                I'm assailed by it,
        and closer to air
                            than,
    she comes
        and she is always, she
    is never in the wind, I recognize
    what the wind is for, jests,
    she avails herself from the
    generalities of sun,

            reconstructs its self at the window,
    loosening the shards of broken ray, and
    then sewing each back

                photon by photon
    of yellow shard, can you imagine the
    heat at its fingers? poor sun,

and brown mares no less,
run their course; halt, at the lip of
stream, pour in gestures to drink –
         at the precise
gut of incision, and
         she hurts me,
and appears
hurt
         in me,

                  fine white flour, wind turning
                  the giant millstones,

                  which you of I is so different,
         our history requires these intemperate
         collisions? –

         if the seas were not insufferable,
                  you'd have them tiled cerulean
                  and then you do,

                  knowing full well these steeds
         will not have come any farther than their
         full course run dry,

                  will have
         ripped me from the ground
         so thoroughly,

                  as if thick horses
                           from a winch,

                  but say I break towards the
         moon, or like some prisoner's escape,
         your raven's dark hounds still bind us –

Dearest, acquiesce,

      I'll build you a house to hang
      all of your instruments, decanter,
      full or loathsome –

      make a rude noose of yourself,
      tip-toe   in & cut myself down if you
      ask me, I'll not go,

           and perhaps, after the fingers
      are tired & swollen –

      mirror of vision gone,
          mute trellis,

     and it will take its course back
                    to the Euphrates,
find the old man there, let's for the sun at the
window, and greet him, wind at the door, it knocks,
and air sweet air, and sleep you girl, back
with the raven,
          a brocade
              qanoun

Coffee Season

We go for oranges
or for cinnamon, we
go with Spring to
Aunty Margaret's

We go with luminosity,
and with reasons, November
as good as any other

If October falls or
resonates more strongly;
who cares about September
or why we miss the evenings

In Summer we go
a-going, and we go quickly,
and at half-past

We go as bridges
and make poems with
our good crossing

We go for coffee, rip the packets
and we go with slurping
throughout the year

Aunty Margaret has a
red dress, the stove's
begonia and bumble-bee

But here December reaches
and there is February from the East,
we go for seasons and tinny spoons
for stirring cinnamon and lemon rind

Who cares whatever for
poetry, we have our cups
and flip them upside down –

Aunty Margaret reads them
and we leave to come back round

Driving Towards Gethsemane

It is with apprehension
that I leave this grove
of olive trees

In the morning
they will come to
take you away

But then, it
has always been
this way –

I hope the spirits you
die for

will touch you
at very least

like the way your lip
quivered when I placed
my fingers beneath your
skirt

on our drive
towards Gethsemane
somewhere between love
and faith now lost

Landscape & Other Voices

Thirty-Three Beads on a String

for Iraq

1

I woke from the nightmare
of a gutted *maqam*.

2

Not because I have
not yet bled my life

in yellow, but because
minarets sky downwards,
looking for purple births.

3

One burly buffalo
shrouded in hooves
and hot breath.

4

Because the skin
is not yet numb,

and the lights
are not flickering,

I will continue to sip
at my hot tea, and stare
at the dust coloured noon.

5

One white *disdasha* screams
with the brilliance of red.

6

Can you hear them —
the melodious intent, the
glimmering oud in their eyes?

7

Faith, stitch by seam,
a garment I have sewn
to my skin.

8

Whatever remains of Al-Gubbenchi's
1932 Cairo studio recording, lives
between the old cobble-stoned quarter,
and my still-warm mahogany ear.

9

I should've gotten
up to shake his hand,

this uncomfortable tension
between me and God.

10

Medina, its streets adorned
with smells from the bazaar, yet
I have chosen to adorn myself
in the still concrete of columns.

11

I'm for the transcription
of the Arabic – sweet spread
over toast, a dark syrup from
dates.

12

Last night Al-Gubbenchi
dreamt of his father's fallen
tooth.

13

In the morning he howled
a song in the name of his father;
Iraq's new fathers weep at
the birth of their sons.

14

Do not cry for Leila or for Hind,
but drink the red wine, and grow
your love doubly, one for the ruby
in the cup, the other for its rouge
upon your cheek.[7]

15

Bombs raked the eyes of the
sleeping Assyrian gods.

16

As if it were only a sandbox,
a few worthless grains of sand.

17

I'll cut for you the last swath
of blue from the sky, sever my
hand if you'll let me

but for five minutes more,
leave me to sleep without the
knowledge of war.

18

A qanoun weeps
near the funeral of music.

19

Having been occupied,
notes mourn for the
loss of their song.

20

I'm for a concert of horses;
the origin of gazelles leapt up
from the heart of Al-Gubbenchi.

21

Had you made small steps into
the desert inside us, or listened
for the guttural lodged deep within
our throats, you would have come
bearing gifts.

22

I have nothing in red
that I would not abide
in green.

23

Al-Mutanabbi wrote the
heart of our silken *tarab*;
what need have we for you?

24

No poem is ever enough red –
but that it's blood might river
through the life of its people.

25

beneath the desert-sun,
a cage in Abu Ghraib,
one man by one man by one man,
breathe six

26

Thousands of tons rung
sonorous from the sky.

Where is god?

27

Black eyed woman,
the street-dogs are running
wild, will you save me?

28

Simple white ignorance:
even the desert has gone into hiding.

29

There is no more meaning
here than the crested moon
holds towards a dying grove
of date trees.

30

I'm for the transcription
of the Arabic – *za'tar zate*
over fire-baked bread.

31

The twin rivers have already
carved for us a history, our poets
have already explained to us
the desert; by what right have
you come ?

32

Who of you has seen
the rustic crane in the tree,
no chimes, but for its delicate
wide beak, ushers an intemperate
reprieve.

33

Thirty-three beads on a string,
why pretend to know beyond
the presence   of click.

North by Fort McMurray

Nine hrs North of Calgary
by car takes you to Fort
McMurray

Two and a half hrs South
of Calgary, by plane, is where
my baby's from, and she's
afraid of the cold –

Here the land runs away from you, I
reach out into the immensity of these figurines –
frozen, twisted and green

        words like muskeg
           and coniferous

      and she's there –
driving into downtown San Francisco
on a Friday night

      the freeways, and streetways,
even they have no room for breathing – there
even the ocean is manned by and iron-truss,

the glitter, the headlights spanning
out beyond the night sky –
      bodies in silk, and low cut denim
rhythms booming in bass   pastel bubble cars
and blue eye shadow make their way
to the night clubs   the supper clubs,
the ladies – and maybe I'll be home
by three she says;

But 30 km North of my grey motel:

a single road carved out
between a scuttle of trees:
old maidens in woody skins,
frost ridden, grey arms bent backwards
chilled in October frost

and the hordes of workers – pipe fitters,
the men moving the earth, cleaving
the land for a dollar –

and the natives from the night before,
I overheard them talking about the drive
between their land and the work site,

over these roads that that have no business
being roads, and when I asked them about the
drive –
thinking about the pick-up,
low on gas, dead of winter,
and what if the river cracks,
the truck dies?

I expected tales of wolves, and frost bite,
huddling alone until you freeze in the night,
and he replied:

"you build a fire,
and bring a winch."

and I look down at my hands, my soft keyboard
clicking hands, and these men driving out through
these trees –

my baby in San Francisco clicking her
heels inside her newest pair of shoes, lighting
her head up with disco balls and Napa Valley
wine

and tomorrow she will call, ask me
about my trip up North by Fort McMurray.

Portrait of the Artist as a Young Immigrant Arab

in mornin time I *pbud* my shoez,
I *pbud* my brown shoez on,
but first you know, I pbud my *banz*,
and then I go for work

after, bus is come, I see many times
beautiful girl, I lookin at them, but
they shy from me, and not talk'in

in work I sittin from my desk,
I work Word & Microsoft, I *pbud*
stable on *baber* and file him

after I break, I checkin my email
then phonin my old-time girl, but she
tired from me, and too much busy,

I say her I love you,
she say me, I love you too,
but you acting too much like child

after work is finish, I go again
in bus – I lookin at beoble, & mostly
they botherin me, too much sad & dull,
they lookin like old brown shoez,

but then I thinkin, they workin hard,
they go home, and havin wife and kidz,
and everyday needin money, and tired,
and life it is not easy – after, I thinkin
some more – I admire them

in bus sometime, mostly habbening
from girl, I get idea because she put her
foot like this, or wear her face in the side,
so I thinkin I like to write boem from her,

then I pbud bell, and bus is finish,
I walkin my house, take shoez, take
banz, and put *disdasha* for house,
is more comfort

I pbut music, sip chai, and sittin
in my chair, and everybody is say,
why you listen to this sad music –

and when emotion is comin s-trong
I go in write

I like to be boet, but I scare – but in
my heart, you know – it is not easy –
you have to pbud ben on baber too much,
maybe then you getting little good;

after I writin, is very late, and I gettin too
much tired, and there is workin tomorrow
morning, so I wash and go for bed

lying down, sometimes, I thinkin too much –
about today and tomorrow and fewjur and bast,
and I makin life too much complicate because
I thinkin right-in-now, and then I banic –

after I thinkin some more, and tellin myself,
wait, now is life, you have to put your banz,
not just for today, but everyday, for many yearz,
you have to pbut your banz –

and then is comin, little by little (*yewash, yewash*) –
I have good job-in-now, I have mother and father
whoez loves me, and lotz good family and friendz

and healthy like horse – and you know, sometime
life is sad, and sometime danger, and too much sexy,
but this is life – like this, like that – so mostly habby,
I closin my eyez, and thinkin tomorrow, which banz.

Leaving Iraq, Entering Alberta

Seems my interest there had
less to do with the place than with
my inhabiting it; yet there were
sublime moments, there and after,
as if the sun had been borne right
all along.

These bouts pass too infrequently,
remembering that sadness motions for
the Aya Sofia, or the Tower of Babil.
My great grandmother knelt to pray
in a 5th century monastery, the Dayr
Zafaran. It still stands there, despite
their murderers, and their murderers
after – before Christmas, she stomps
wine from red Mardilli grapes.

This then, is the story of a non-City
swept off of the Mediterranean Sea.
The foothills rose up to greet her outcry,
her mountains rose up from the earth.
Those gulls arcing, grey and high,
above turquoise minarets, forgotten
souls waiting for the current, or the
breath of some god to ordain them.

There is also the story of this prodigal
son, and the sumptuous blonde wriggling
beside me – and it was either go and make
something of your talents, or slink inside
her jiggly clefts. I chose the blonde. There
has been no rejoinder, dreams go, and I
miss them.

Why bother fiddling with the map and
compass? The desert will save us – whispers
love, broken glass, a chimera, or lizard creeps.
Outside father returns from work, wipes the
tired from his eyes, and we are knee-high
pressed against the window, the smile in his
eyes, we are these gifts to him – two fretless
chords, the Tigris and the Bow. What for the
clutter of maps, the desert, that this small
house might see us through it; father asleep
on the floor – we, the current through his life.

And drink the Euphrates – I'm for the
sun, and discourse, a field at talk with
its horse. What need do I have for war,
what concern do I carry for names, how
pure is the light in this dark, a city asleep,
one small boy, two tunnels.

Impressions from Turkish folk songs
afford me tiny doorways. Their delicate
pastoral – white goat's cheese spread over
fire baked bread, or supine naps under a
cypress. Evening kisses both cheeks, and
we go with loose stomping. After dinner
we wipe our mouths against the worn
ends of this city, beyond this table-cloth.

Last night a small boy fell in the creek
and drowned. I go to diners and to pubs,
to market, and for breakfasts. I order my
eggs runny, slurp my coffee among friends.
And I cannot begin to see how an entire city

could occupy the space of one small plate;
and sisters for whom we must find good men
to marry, and if we don't who will? Istanbul
doesn't wait, exhales its traffic, these polluted
ceilings, noises crossing mountains. And for
the small boy who drowned in the creek last
night there is decomposition.

I've seen Alberta gone yellow in fractures
of wheat, pressed the flaxen of every drum
between my sleepy fingers; sucked dawn
out of the Iraqi maqam, the Shat El Arab, a
window with no perimeter. I swam for its
farthest reaches, forgetting the border. Closer
still, I crawled beneath the heavy arm of my
father, these mountains North of Kirkuk, his
breath like a geyser hot against my neck. Here
in the Athabasca Tar Sands, all of the oil in
the world trapped frozen in the ground. Not
for its centuries' commerce, or these Northern
latitudes; but for a small boy careful not to
wake the city beside him, and still lives there.

I could not drain the blood from Lake Van.
The sky's an ocean we drive up, swallows us,
this isolation, and we warm to the Rockies, to
clarity, the foot of these mountains. We laugh
the way down, sure – but say you take two
brothers, place them on either side of their
father, shoot one, then the other – whose father
will have died from the shock. March countless
elegies into the Syrian sun, leaving Turkey,
entering Alberta, beautiful expansive sky.

My Grandfather, a tinsmith, dissapeared
somewhere between Mardin and Northern
Iraq. His reasons have dug us a womb deep
in the snow. We are all there, in Canada,
waiting for an unearthed Assyrian clay
tablet, or an inscription of his borders.

Alberta thaws around an old brown post.
Indexes of forgotten space, soundless days
like when you swore to me an owl, of an old
Fort, upon entering, upon leaving. Outside,
a continent's distance away, Ankara at 3:00
AM. Here in this city the cars and buses make
more noise than all of my remembering aloud,
weave contrapuntal sounds. I get up to shut the
noise, return to sit with plastic thongs. I look
in the mirror, a face in this city begins.

The Thursday's spilled on the floor. Poems
hung on coat-racks. Winter warming under
skirts near the bar. Do you remember the
Saturdays melting? I meant to keep a portrait
of Tuesday, your eyes ruddy with laughter –
were they blue? As she wipes our best words
clean off the table, turns for the promise of
another chilled pint.

In what country is my wife sleeping now?
Say that I know it, say that I can stitch her
soul along the contours of her body, backwards.
I can drum up from the loose patterns of her
hair some isolated tremor of her childhood,
that I know her latitude and longitude so well

that landing is both effortless and a thrill.
Perhaps, at best, this is a lie; perhaps all I am
to her is the portion of the story which she has
allowed – her Northerns, her Southerns, this
shut-eyed city asleep. I hear her breathe, in–out.

I pray for the hour of our absolution, her hair over
candle-blue hills. Last night we two by the fire, and
her father will be incensed if she is not back by noon,
not because he lacks understanding, or that we care
less for the history of Antakya, but that we too have
been to the first church, a grassy swath of moon,
fairway #7, where Peter carved out God against the
side of a mountain; made himself a brick in the temple
of Christ. Two thousand years later, Muslim leaving
Jew, leaving the warmth of our fire, where only a few
tourists will have climbed. No prayer ever guts itself
into the flesh like a whip because prayer can only go
so far without gods. But we two, having found fire,
and fuel enough to fill volumes.

I have thought myself to be an Iraqi-Canadian.
Rather Aramean, who spoke with Christ, became
Arabized, borne to Canada by way of Baghdad.
I speak little of the Arabic: In *Sha'Allah*, *Marhaba*,
Zane. I have spent more hours ripping ice than there
are grains in the sand, guitars being among some of
my closest of friends, whom I love more with each
pint. If my prairies sound semitic, or the colour of my
city is olive, whose borders are they? Mother and
Father brought us love all the way from there, to
give it here, and bombs continue. Arctic terns turn
by night the full sweep of the poles: Iraq in the throat
of the singer's maqam, or Alberta purple-black
on a sunlit crow.

My brother these warriors pour down
into the valley like heavy rains; Assyria,
Babylonia, white columns flush with
memory, mortar by sound. My brother,
why do you worry? Worry is like a donkey
without a road. These warriors like heavy
rains, a road between us.

Leaving Iraq, entering Alberta, Autumn falls
contrapuntal on a leaf. No matter my sorrow or
elation, afflictions still forged by a tinsmith – a
summer that bled, a winter that hurts; and for a
magpie stalled in the snow, Mesopotamia waits
for further appropriations; or new farmers to till
inside their meaning. My narrative last seen leaving
the unseen self, moves Westward. Nobody told me
that a country can swallow you whole, and expects
you to do the same. The self carves its face from
a poplar. And driving along Highway 22X, South
of Calgary, having much less to do with this place,
than with my story growing inside it.

Asking Iraq to Comply

(written prior to the U.S. invasion of Iraq on 21 March 2003)

A decade ago the words: comply comply comply,
hundreds of thousands of Iraqi men dead, generations
of Iraqi children sanctioned to graves, and still, comply comply
comply, how much death is ever enough compliance? how
do you go about desecrating with bombs
on the birthplace of Abraham, of Ishmael and Isaac,
of Arab and Jew, of Christian and Muslim,
of Koran and the Bible?
Iraq is the world's first love poem,
is the Epic of Gilgamesh scribed onto tablets
three millennia ago, is Sumerian
is Akkadian is the first written language,
the first poetry, the first pottery –
Iraq is Assyrian, is Mede, is Persian,
is Babylonian, is the origins of human
narrative flowing into the Tigris,
flowing out of the Euphrates,
flowing into Eden, into Genesis,
into Adam and into Eve, into Ur and its Kings;
Iraq spans the lives of the oldest traditions,
the Marsh Arabs, "Ma'dan," who
for centuries thrived off the world's first
irrigation canals, now forced to irrigate
plutonium into their crops, into their children,
dropped by planes, dropped by thousands
and thousands of sortie campaigns
in the name of compliance, dropped by America;
Iraq is the first science, the first math, "al-jabr,"
"algebra" meaning "restoration";
Iraq is the first universities – "madrassa"
of once glorious Baghdad,
the first words brought together
in the first library of Assurbanipal,

in that first city of light at Nineveh;
Iraq is the Bedouin and his proud history,
is his honor and loyalty travelling through
the first caravans on camels,
the first trade routes bringing coffee,
bringing spices, bringing celebration of foods
laid out among family and friends;
Iraq is the first music, the first guitar,
"al-ud," brought into Europe with the first translations
from the Greek, from the Latin, from Aristotle
and Plato, written into Arabic,
written from the Aramaic,
the language of Christ,
Iraq is the first Christians of the East,
who lived among Muslims, together as Arabs,
now forced to comply, to line up for rations,
to beg in the streets of Iraq,
the once-learned center of the Abbasids, of al-Rashid;
the first written history of the middle ages is Iraq,
the bearers of medicines and astronomies,
of logarithms and philosophies;
Iraq is Chaldaeans and Kurds, Nestorians
and Turkmen, is the place of the first Gods,
the first laws of Hammurabi's code giving
order to the first societies – now forced to comply,
the place of the first Kings saying to their sons
over 3000 yrs ago, "how long will it be necessary
for us to continually guide you?"
is like my father saying to me, is like all parents
forever worried and hopeful about the future of
their children – is Iraq saying now,
so how? how do you go about demanding
compliance, without first having made amends?

Seasons of the Imperial Imagination

(a fugue)

He: I wanted to get outside of it, so
that I could get right side of the notes
again. None of the levity that went out
in the blood-letting. I wanted to give
you the romantic in a picture made
ugly made beautiful, or the something
Southerly in the voice of a girl.

She: Is not departure a drive
through lush-oak? Green, their arms
dangling and long, thatched intersections
we weave, the kind of world you'd build
your house beneath.

          And if some intangible
beauty should sit itself down, sunshine.
Why the insistence of doom, terror
in the eyes?

I am alive!

          He is alive
for finding me alive.

          Has kissed me this boy,
this freedom upon my cheek, and cries
for the light of his mother.

Chorus:

Inside—
the columns,
wind
towering
over the
leaves that
sway in the sun.
Licked the
sleeve

of night.
And I will
go to my
grave
wanting
for a song
that is neither
in me
nor of me.
The ascension
of pianos
keyed up
inside.

He: But to go again
             into the rain. To peel back
             the skin from each blue
             kernel of rain.

She: Not yours to murder

             Rather a
             willingness to give grief
             its terse percussion.

He: Under bodies
             I have had loves read in
             poems, proverbs as fathers,
             countries for gods.

             But for a drink! –
             For a rock thundery sound!

             They who have
             no discourse, they have all
             of them large appetites, so
             we feed them:

             a grave,

a piano,
wanton fingers like
manicured gods. A box
of sunny clefts.

Here! – here is the
depth of my feeling – then
let me govern it.

She:　　　　A black man's blues, or
sad Italian's heavy libretto. Opera
has a house, but none for me. I'm
given to a tree.

He:　　　　I make love to my
sundry rotations.

She:　　　　You will be its shoe-
shine boy, you will be spit-shine
for a grain or two of its sand, fade
and then fade.

He:　　I like a woman –
looms over sunset,
and no tears, and warms me. The eternal
is all I want from you, brightly poured
from the night –

Chorus:

or you
remain
my sickle,
my dove.
You slice
the night,
sound left
from thousands
of leavings

of light.
Light that
left me
Pluto-white
and distant.
You are key
after key, I
am one mad-
man on a
park-bench.
You don't
believe me?
then watch
the light ripple
across my
face, leaves
me, breast
& after
hip, sweet
in the hurt
of your
thigh, has
song in it,
& noose
all around,
& tall, a leg
so fine—

He: I go. And then achingly, I
go again. And this is no complaint,
but what moon circles knowing it
must circle again?

She: You are no more
well off than stone, bit of sunlight.
The water rises against you.

He: There goes the wind, so
      how shall I catch it? –

   Past the village
      there is a river.
   I am leaving the place of your
   white legs splashing and kicking
   at the water's edge.

   If your father
      only knew your cheek
   was my moon, he'd have slaughtered
   the fattest sheep then fed me
   the meat from his fingers.

     The wind long,
   moon quivers, I have eyes
   for other planets,
      save me
         a flute,

     A musket. A country
   up in its trousers storms through
   a crag in the granite

She: All of your
   knights, rode in through
   the gates of Jerusalem.

He: And inside
   the flute: a guitar,

      inside the guitar,
        a horse.

She: As if a blind man
   has never wept for a vision
   of Venus.

He: Here, here is the thick
of its blood! Here is the sky's
rotation –

She: As if god has never
gone down to bathe in the turbulent
boom of Jupiter's red-eye.

Chorus:

The ant
that looms
in the
grass,
mint-blade
between
its jaw.

She: There's Io, Pluto
           white & distant.

He: I cannot feel my fingers
for the chill of late November –

Chorus:

thrum`pa
pa`pum tum

He: and for a long time
sounds like the notes from
muffled instruments.

Nature: Morning's
consequence rises on
a cactus.

He: But to get inside of it? –

Nature: A promise
once made in the garden,
inlay of stones, a caterpillar
munches on a leaf,
              birds
from lurch
              to arc,
              Ants who would
murder for a crumb. All of
the dandelions have shed
their yellow for white

She: Bach is sealed
tightly into orange jars –
What marmalade might
we find there?

Nature: A navy-blue chill has
stalled atop the chimney stacks, plucked
the cars from their streets – even the
              spruces have uttered an oboe's
              prayer.

Chorus:

La ilaha ila Allah
La ilaha ila Allah

Nature: Summer's lids
hacked by hungry mowers;

He: Here! Here is wind
from under hammock!

Nature: the little flecks
of mint, jade instances
of the wind
              scattered under
hedges, and left for
busy gnats.

Chorus:

Autumn
plucks
the keys
in trees,
as Glenn
Gould
would
wind them,
laughs a
ripe bouquet
of clavichord,
and goes
its dread
macabre.

Nature: Suddenly, a leaf
has wind: its trickle across
the sill.
        Asleep, only in sleep
lies winter, the promise of ice
& of time.

Chorus:

ta`thrum
ta`tum tum

Nature: These apt portions
of the palette: fresh-clipped green,
kettle-red, or copper-blue. But for the rue
left singing at the bottom of the seasonal
pot: My belly spooning for the last bits
of stew.

        Music over ice. Light mixing
with the delicate white. A season for winter.
Trees in a field with the promise of sound.

He: After the paint dries, and the
twilight loosens, after the tendrils and
bits of pollen are empty, who will fill
our coffee cups?

She: Not for myth,
or a shadow, not in levity
drawn up from the cosmos.

           But for jam & blue
kites, for an ounce of the fresh
squeezed South!

Chorus:

There is
more of Bach
in a child's
kazoo,
And I will
go to my
grave
wanting
for a song
that is
neither in
me, nor of
me, but
warmth
from the
jacket
of night.

He: Winter is made
happiest with your concert
of boots in the snow.

Nature: November leans
against the side of the moon. And if you have
stuffed more of December inside your pockets,
then I hope you will have left some room
for orange.

She: That you
will have been there: –
a drive through lush-oak!

Nature: November yielding
to August, turns to May –
Winter's cobalt
        frozen on a stone.

Afterword

That I know of another narrative has meant everything to me. That I have tried to grasp its palpable heft, its ability to move the author beyond place and time has given me new possibility. Perhaps that's what any good poem should do. Perhaps the most valuable thing any writer can do is study the movement of words in history, how they have begun, from where, how they have found a place inside him, and with what force they will continue to move.

One can, I suppose, assume the words given him. But what of the shape of the individual, what of the fit, and why should one conform to any deliberate or arbitrary demarcation rather than struggle with continual vigour? For what remains of the author, or the individual, who is orphaned, or rather subsumed by his words?

And what of those who have complacently, or unknowingly, without agitation, without *ijtihad* (that is, without independent or analytical thought achieved through personal commitment and effort), placed themselves inside of an overarching narrative, without recourse to possibility, save for what is given them? And what rough monster Iraq must now seem under the auspices of such a narrator.

A grand narrative has been constructed at the expense of the Iraqi people, but a more vigorous assessment might have challenged the ethics and validity behind this narrative, even of its right to exist, let alone its implementation. Yet it persists, and with what sweeping distortion. The world entertains this bed time story, only for Iraq, it is a nightmare.

There is another Iraq. Other narratives have arrived from the Arab world bringing, whether we would acknowledge them or not, great benefit to humanity; other lineages have come in peace and in tolerance, stories that have revealed to us that the Iraqi people are also "forever worried and hopeful about the future of their children."

Though this new publication of *Taqsim* will mean nothing to the history and suffering of the Iraqi people—it is another narrative. What will mean a good deal, however, is if enough people struggle to renew and make peace with those other narratives, many already set down millennia ago by Iraq, its writers, poets, history, culture, and by its people. That the Tigris and the Euphrates continue to flow is testament enough—their tributaries will continue to cultivate, so long as people will read them.

Endnotes:

1   In Arabic music, free-form melodic improvisation,
    performed by solo voice or on a solo instrument
    (oud)
2   A long-neck string instrument similar to the oud,
    native to the regions of Turkey and Kurdistan
3   "asik"or "ozan" poet singers, or bards in the regions
    of Turkey and Kurdistan
4   anise flavored alcohol of the Middle East
5   In Iraq one of several complex musical scales,
    or forms, typically associated with a specific
    tone or mood.
6   A thirty string Middle Eastern instrument
    similar to the zither.
7   A loose translation from the "Wine Songs" of
    Abu Nuwas

Zaid Shlah's poetry is as "multifoliate" as Yeats' rose in its blending of contemporary voice with the ancient traditions of Iraqi and Arabic poetry and music. He is as much at home with the expansive Qasida tradition as with the work of Ezra Pound, William Carlos Williams, and Derek Walcott. Richly lyrical and sensual ("the apple tree promenading its / red treasure, and twig-light just coming on"), his work brings us to a world that feels immediately familiar because so close to the mind's famous eye.

~ *Paul Hoover*

Zaid Shlah's *Taqsim* sings! This book's gripping melancholy and unique resonance in the face of departure and loss is tough and exciting, it tells us to "leave the river, leave the grass, leave the gaze….the words rooting in your eyes, leave the sun…its lie – go and be something beautiful." Shlah takes us to the radiance of Arab history, cultures, religions while "driving along Highway 22X, South of Calgary, having much less to do with [the] place, than with the story growing inside it." These poems confess and connect us to the turbulent mystery of beauty and the quiet voice of the world.

~ *Nathalie Handal*

Mark Gould

A native Calgarian, Zaid Shlah now resides in Walnut Creek, CA with his wife Randa. He obtained his MA in English from San Francisco State University. His poetry has appeared in literary magazines and journals in both Canada and the United States. Most recently he was awarded the American Academy of Poets Award. Zaid teaches in Walnut Creek, and lectures at New College of California.